INTRODUCTION

Quirky, cozy, and architecturally unmistakable, A-Frames were all the rage back in the mid-century era. Small in stature but brimming with character, these homes often served as a point of much-needed respite from the fast pace of modern-day life. Recently, these unique cabins have resurged as an iconic figure of simpler times and have found their way into the hearts of home owners and travelers alike. Nowadays, the community of A-Frame aficionados are found in all corners of the country, and we've found ourselves among that inner triangle.

In 2020, we purchased our first A-Frame in Wilmington, Vermont, with the idea of adding this special spot to Wildwood Collective, our curated collection of vacation rental properties. The house, which we now lovingly call The Alpine A-Frame, was our entryway into the amazingly supportive, encouraging and exciting A-Frame community. The home and our story are shared within the pages of this book, as well as twelve other perfect A-Frames.

From a ship-inspired cabin perched above the rocky Maine coastline to a sleek, modern masterpiece under the towering redwoods of the Pacific Northwest, this coloring book serves to celebrate these wonderfully unique and picture-perfect homes. What's more, all of the houses that appear in the first volume of The A-Frame Coloring Book are available to rent on short-term vacation rental sites (like Airbnb and VRBO), making each page a potential getaway destination.

One last note, we want to thank all of our wonderful A-Frame community members who contributed their lovely homes to this project. We hope this book brings you joy, not only to color but perhaps also plan your next vacation!

And if you're feeling colorful, be sure to tag #aframecoloringbook in your post. We'd love to see what you create!

All the /\ :

Lauren Hudson & Chris Krieger

WILDWOOD COLLECTIVE

www.wildwoodcollective.co

@wildwoodcollective.co

THE A-FRAMES

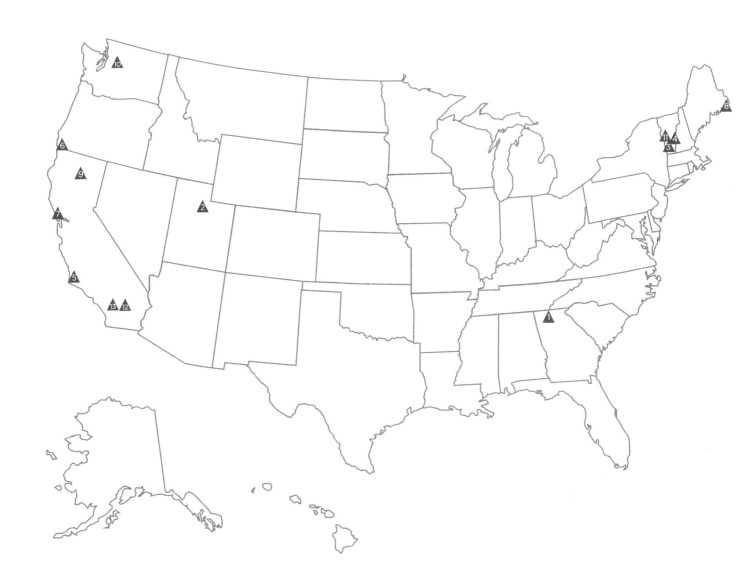

1. A-FRAME CHALET

2. A-FRAME HAUS

3. THE ALPINE A-FRAME

4. BLACK A-FRAME VERMONT

5. BOHO A-FRAME

6. CEDAR BLOOM A-FRAME

7. INVERNESS A-FRAME

8. PROWHOUSE

9. THE TREEHOUSE

10. TYE HAUS

11. THE VERMONT A-FRAME

12. WHISKEY RIDGE CHALET

13. THE WILSON HAUS

△

A-FRAME
CHALET

LOCATION: Ellijay, GA
YEAR BUILT: 1973
OWNERS: Roanna Bales & Thomas Akin
INSTAGRAM: @aframechalet
PHOTO CREDIT: Desmond Jones

WHAT MAKES YOUR HOUSE SPECIAL?

I have always dreamt of owning a 1970's A-Frame and very few of them exist in the north Georgia mountains. We think our cabin is special because we have the most magical sunsets over the mountains, and during the summer months it's like living in a treehouse. At night I love when the warm wood walls glow from the soft lighting and it feels like a big giant hug! Our A-Frame is perfect for experiencing all the seasons of the north Georgia mountains!

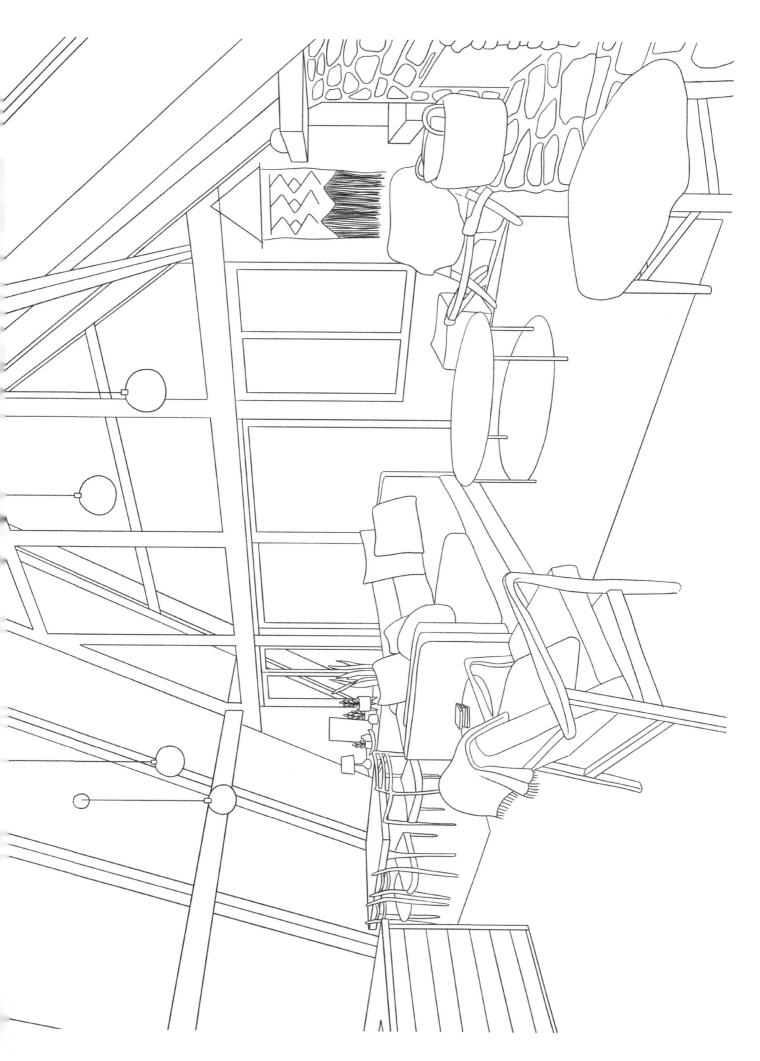

△

A-FRAME HAUS

LOCATION: Heber Valley, Utah
YEAR BUILT: 1989
OWNERS: Kara James
INSTAGRAM: @aframehaus
PHOTO CREDIT: Kate Osborne
WEBSITE: https://aframehaus.com/

WHAT MAKES YOUR HOUSE SPECIAL?

Our grandpa built this cabin over 30 years ago as a place of solitude to write music and meditate. We feel so lucky to be carrying on his legacy by sharing this haven in the mountains with others!

△

THE ALPINE
A-FRAME

LOCATION: Wilmington, VT
YEAR BUILT: 1958
OWNERS: Lauren Hudson & Chris Krieger (owners of Wildwood Collective)
INSTAGRAM: @alpineaframevt
PHOTO CREDIT: Lauren Hudson & Chris Krieger // Ethan Abitz
WEBSITE: www.wildwoodcollective.co

WHAT MAKES YOUR HOUSE SPECIAL?

Ever since we got into the vacation rental business in 2017, we had been on the lookout for a special "A" to call our own. In 2020, we finally became the proud owners of this little blue gem, The Alpine A-Frame. Given our love for midcentury modern design, we had a blast transforming this A-frame to an era-appropriate throwback. Every item in the house was chosen with care. The Alpine A-Frame sits nestled between Lake Raponda and Mount Snow, making it the perfect four-season Vermont escape.

△

BLACK A-FRAME VERMONT

LOCATION: West Wardsboro, VT
YEAR BUILT: ~1950
OWNERS: Jody Mead
INSTAGRAM: @blackaframevt
PHOTO CREDIT: Jody Mead

WHAT MAKES YOUR HOUSE SPECIAL?

It's the perfect escape - on 7+ private acres with a trail to access the brook below the house/ nestled between Stratton and Mt Snow - and the road is "Smead" and my daughters name is Skylar / last name mead so it seemed meant to be!

△

BOHO A-FRAME

LOCATION: Los Osos, CA
YEAR BUILT: 1954
OWNERS: Candice and Wyatt Childers
INSTAGRAM: @boho_aframe
PHOTO CREDIT: Candice and Wyatt Childers

WHAT MAKES YOUR HOUSE SPECIAL?

Our A-Frame Airbnb isn't your typical cabin because it's just minutes from the beach. We have chosen to decorate with a bohemian vibe instead of traditional cabin decor. It's a destination for those that seek a cabin experience by the sea.

△

CEDAR BLOOM A-FRAME

LOCATION: Cave Junction, OR
YEAR BUILT: 2017
OWNERS: Mea, Agustin & Naia
INSTAGRAM: @cedarbloomfarm
PHOTO CREDIT: Mea, Agustin & Naia
WEBSITE: https://www.cedarbloomfarm.com/

WHAT MAKES YOUR HOUSE SPECIAL?

The A-Frames at Cedar Bloom are the perfect way to up your camping experience. With all the amenities that Cedar Bloom has to offer, these tiny A-Frames add to the perfect Glamping weekend. The side of the A-Frame opens up so that you can feel the essence of the outdoors while still sleeping in a cozy bed inside. Each A-frame is about 100 sf inside making it the coziest tiny home.

△

INVERNESS A-FRAME

LOCATION: West Marin, California
YEAR BUILT: 1973
INSTAGRAM: @invernessaframe
PHOTO CREDIT: Tom Storey // Kat Alves
WEBSITE: https://invernessaframe.com/

WHAT MAKES YOUR HOUSE SPECIAL?

Rustic Modern A-Frame lovingly renovated by BLYTHE DESIGN CO. It it is a creative gathering space that hosts arts workshops, overnight guests, and nature therapy retreats - all while serving as the owner's forested home by the seashore.

△

PROWHOUSE

LOCATION: Machiasport, ME
YEAR BUILT: 2001
OWNERS: Rich and Julie Rose
PHOTO CREDIT: Rich Rose

WHAT MAKES YOUR HOUSE SPECIAL?

Each morning in Maine some of the sun's first rays bathe the East-facing facade of the Prowhouse. Designed to evoke a ship, and perched high up on a cliff covered in blueberries, the Prowhouse quietly overlooks Howard Cove, home to bald eagles, harbor porpoise, and unique Jasper Beach, a pebble-collector's paradise.

△

THE TREEHOUSE

LOCATION: Lakehead, CA
YEAR BUILT: 1973
OWNERS: Madison and Cees Hofman
INSTAGRAM: @treehouseaframe
PHOTO CREDIT: Madison and Cees Hofman
WEBSITE: https://treehouse.ourvie.com/

WHAT MAKES YOUR HOUSE SPECIAL?

Built on stilts, the A-Frame looks as if it is in the trees! A dreamy A-Frame cabin nestled in four wooded acres overlooking Shasta Lake. The deck looks out over the valley with breathtaking views of mountain peaks, granite cliffs and Hirz Bay. Located in the middle of thousands of acres of National Forest, and right between 3 beautiful National Parks – Lassen Volcanic, Redwood, and Crater Lake.

△

TYE HAUS

LOCATION: Skykomish, WA
YEAR BUILT: 1978
OWNERS: Tom & Sarah
INSTAGRAM: @tyehaus
PHOTO CREDIT: Kyle Smith (@dipsauce)
WEBSITE: http://tyerivercabinco.com/

WHAT MAKES YOUR HOUSE SPECIAL?

Located about an hour from Seattle, Washington, Tye Haus A-Frame cabin is surrounded by some of the best hikes in the Pacific Northwest and offers excellent access to skiing, fishing and mountain biking.

△

THE VERMONT A-FRAME

LOCATION: Manchester Center, VT
YEAR BUILT: 1965
OWNERS: Jason Pomeroy & Monique DeLorenzo
INSTAGRAM: @thevermontaframe
PHOTO CREDIT: Pete Curialle & Andrew Pinnella
WEBSITE: https://thevermontaframe.com

WHAT MAKES YOUR HOUSE SPECIAL?

When you open the door, you're met with the unmistakable scent of cedar from the original wall panels, which we decided to leave intact. It's a nod to the era in which the home was built, and it's more welcoming than a candle ever could be. We always recommend starting your day with coffee by the wood stove, and ending your day the same way - just swap the coffee for a cocktail. When you wake up in the morning, take in the sight of the treetops and the sound of the babbling brook in the forest behind you. This house is special because whether for a weekend or a few weeks, it will make you feel at home.

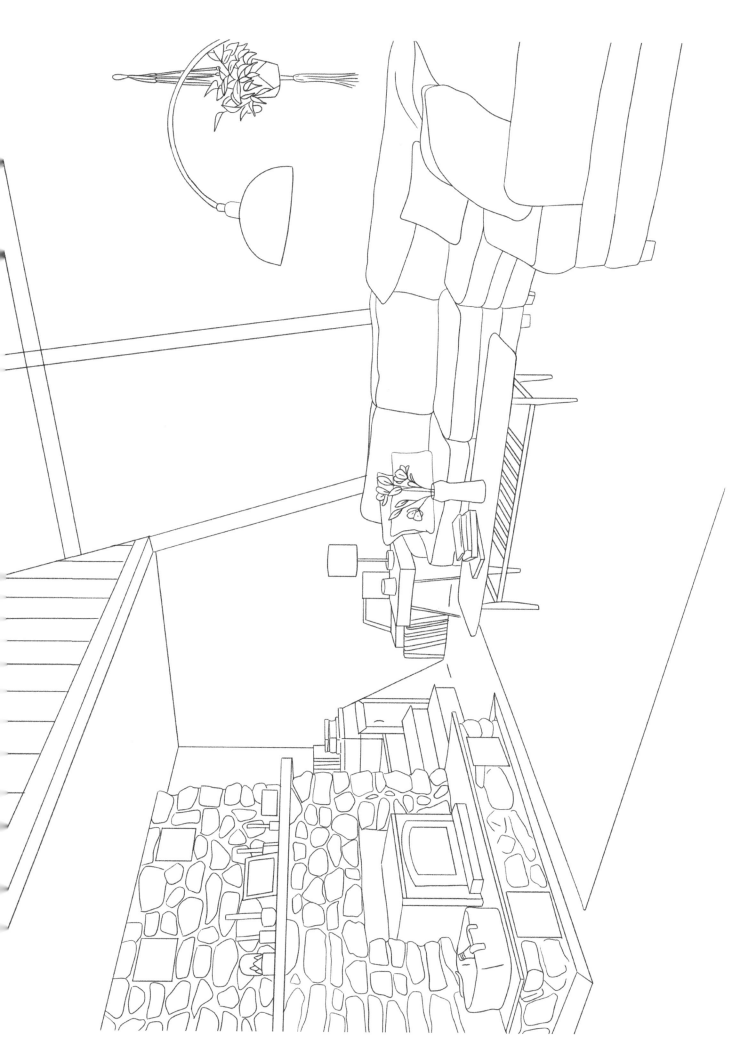

WHISKEY RIDGE CHALET

LOCATION: Big Bear Lake, CA (Moonridge)
YEAR BUILT: 1973
OWNERS: Courtney Poulos, Devin Elston
INSTAGRAM: @WhiskeyRidgeChalet
PHOTO CREDIT: @dirtandglass // @chadwickmalcolm
WEBSITE: https://www.bigbearaframe.com/

WHAT MAKES YOUR HOUSE SPECIAL?

The Cabin is on a quiet cul-de-sac in a lovely area, close to both Resorts and Town but with the feeling of being far away from everything.

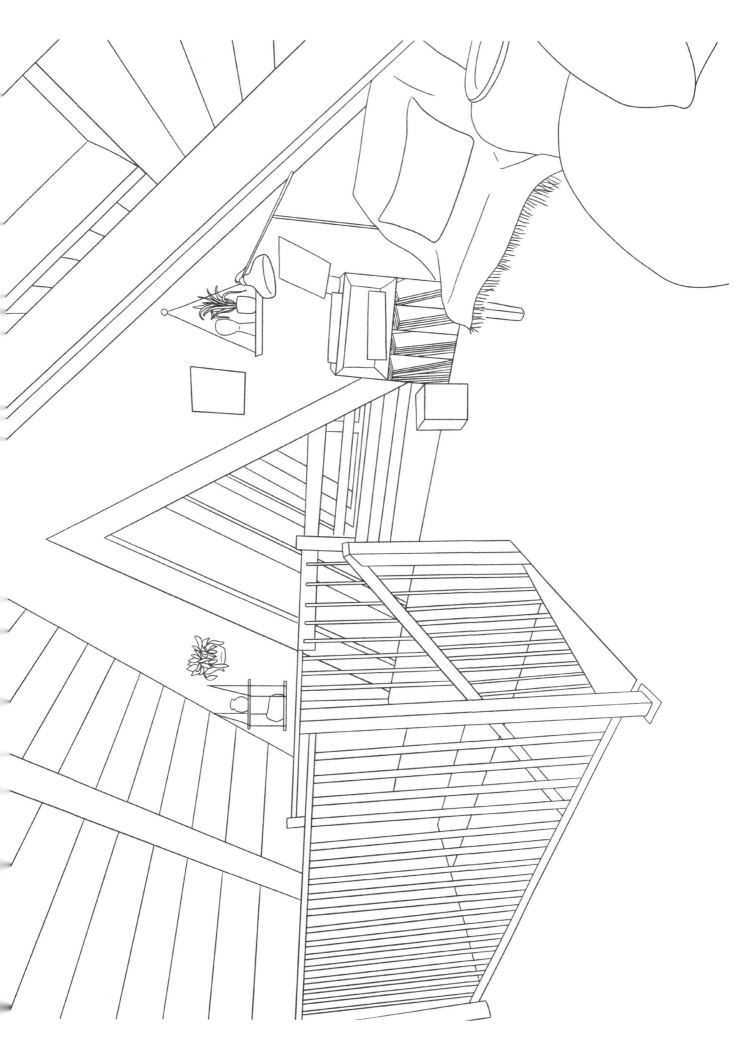

△

THE WILSON HAUS

LOCATION: Lake Arrowhead, CA
YEAR BUILT: 1964
OWNERS: Will & Casie Wilson
INSTAGRAM: @thewilsonhaus
PHOTO CREDIT: @thewilsonhaus
WEBSITE: https://www.thewilsonhaus.com

WHAT MAKES YOUR HOUSE SPECIAL?

The Wilson Haus is a cabin nestled in a quiet cul-de-sac in Lake Arrowhead, CA. As we worked to design our home, we wanted to make sure we created a space parents and their kids could enjoy. From our kid-sized book nook, to the kid's art studio, to Buck our singing reindeer, everything was chosen to keep the whole family entertained and feeling right at home!

Made in the USA
Las Vegas, NV
10 February 2025

17803005R00031